The 12-Month Guide for Becoming a Top Choice Bachelor

by

July Jones & Monty Sharpe

authorHOUSE®

AuthorHouse™
1663 Liberty Drive, Suite 200
Bloomington, IN 47403
www.authorhouse.com
Phone: 1-800-839-8640

First published by AuthorHouse 8/27/2007

ISBN: 978-1-4343-0913-6 (sc)

*Printed in the United States of America
Bloomington, Indiana*

This book is printed on acid-free paper.

The 12-Month Guide for Becoming a Top Choice Bachelor

July Jones & Monty Sharpe

Month 1. *The usual suspects*
Mantra: Be able to recognize the eight types of women and know which is attainable for you.

Month 2. *Look the part, act the part, and be the part*
Mantra: Concentrate on being the person you want to be and not the person you currently are.

Month 3. *Money: There's a thin line between being broke and being a damn fool*
Mantra: Be smarter with your money and keep your financial situation to yourself.

Month 4. *You think you're the driver but you're the butler*
Mantra: Do not be taken advantage of, and experience life on your terms.

Month 5. *Her kids, your burden*
Mantra: Do what's best for you and not for everyone else; do not become a surrogate father unless you want to be.

Month 6. *Running things means never having to say it*
Mantra: When faced with an adverse situation, remain calm, quiet, and concise.

Month 7. *Keep her guessing*
Mantra: Do not allow yourself to get comfortable in the comfort zone; actively pursue perfection.

Month 8. *Do what other brothers won't and go places they don't*
Mantra: Be unique and innovative about where you choose to spend your time.

Month 9. *Winning the "friend" game*
Mantra: Treat people according to who they are, not as you wish them to be.

Month 10. *Know when to bow out gracefully*
Mantra: Do not allow your ego to cloud your better judgment.

Month 11. *Keep your lips closed while keeping hers open*
Mantra: Keep your personal life personal.

Month 12. *Bring your "A" game*
Mantra: Become the top choice bachelor mind, body, and soul.

Who are The Coalition?

Many wonder but few know the truth. The Coalition represents an amalgamation of single and married ultra-successful males who have combined their years of knowledge interacting with the opposite sex into a 12-month guide. A how-to manual which will take an individual from being "a man" to "the man" in 12 short months, step by step. July Jones and Monty Sharpe, two members of The Coalition, have chosen to shed the cloak of anonymity and chronicle the thoughts and philosophies of the single members of the organization. To date, other Coalition members have chosen to remain anonymous.

MONTH 1
The usual suspects

As warfare goes, victory is savored by those who prepare best and those who devise the most effective strategies. It was once said that "practice makes perfect," and when it comes to dealing with women, especially black women, a lot of practice is needed. Sistas are professionals at using the arts of manipulation, reverse psychology, and seduction. Before you realize it, the game is over before it has begun. You're carrying purses and smoking briskets at 6 a.m. for the in-laws coming over for weekend barbeques. We say, "Fuck that, and fuck anyone else who thinks differently about it." But if you are smart, you will maximize your chances of not falling into these traps. No hunter goes into the woods without knowledge of what they're hunting. Studying the ways in which they move, behavior patterns, strengths, weaknesses, and devise strategies to anticipate what move will be made next.

When hunting big game black women, it is crucial to know the various types and which you plan to go after:

Sweetness of the ghetto

If an ass with gold teeth could talk, it would belong to her. All the grit of the cats from around the way with half the brains. A love for malt liquors and tattoos paired with crass sayings and an aura of bad taste, she's always down for late night hype and has been known to go to jail for foolishness — you love her for this, though you will admit it to no one but yourself while fuckin'.

The body

What more need I say? Fellas want to bang her and females want to hate because they wish they had an ass like that and who could blame them? Really she makes ordinary, pedestrian outfits like uniforms and warm-up suits look like video-ho shit; it's amazing! Nice feet, cut calves capped by thighs that pump up and down like engine pistons when she walks, a flat stomach paired with an "ass like whoa" chased with breasts perfectly sized for your hands and a face that could quite frankly look like whatever because your taking whatever she's got for sale…. Her ass had you at hello.

The power broker

High-heeled pumps and a business suit never look better than it does on this woman. Brains with a bangin' body and an attitude to match make her irresistible. She knows it and so do you, so why fight that? Smart enough to smell bullshit coming but still wants to be dominated when the lights go out; this honey likes to fuck you back and will ask, "Do you like that?" She suffers from "glass roof syndrome." She constantly craves validation. Beware: Her needs are as deep as she is fine. Only fully aware Top Choice Bachelors need apply.

The fashionista

If it's hot on the streets or chic in the stores, she's got it on and will not hesitate to tell you how much it costs. Simply put, it takes Prada, Gucci, Louie V, Fendi, Manolo Blahnik, etc. to keep her happy. She has four words she lives by: "Fuck you, pay me." Dinner? Fuck you, pay me. Night on the town? Fuck you, pay me. Head? Fuck you, pay me! Everything comes at a price and often a hefty one: *pay to play.* In exchange for said fees and surcharges, you get a runway quality chick that looks good in designer shit and stilettos. She's sporting the latest, you're financing it, and all you have to show for it is average head and occasional, compensatory pussy … feel special?

The mainstay

She cooks, cleans, gets along with your mother, and

gets freaky on your birthday. She's got a good shape, decent waist, and is overall respectful but always comes up a bit short. And why? Because hard work is not needed to get her. And what does that mean? She is always thankful for what or whom she has. "Mainstay" will never challenge you or ultimately push you to achieve Top Choice Bachelor status. "Mainstay" never requires you to be "on point." She fosters a nature of malingering, and in turn you show subpar skills that will only attract what they will: subpar companions.

Ms. Mix-a-lot

Is she black? Asian? "Blasian?" Caribbean? Italian with a splash of Africa? Whatever she is, or isn't, know that she has your attention. She has an exotic look about her, freakishly curly or ridiculously straight hair, and unnatural proportions that are earmarks of her mixed heritage. There is a hint of confusion surrounding; who could resist? Being of dual heritage, "mix-a-lot" feels pressure from both sides of the fence: not black enough for the sistas, not "whatever" enough for the others. She often is in search of shelter from the storm while being stacked with a bad ass body and hazel eyes. APPROACH WITH CAUTION. Beauty comes at a cost; oftentimes, her search for comfort leads to neurosis. "Mix-a-lot" has a potential for being too needy; once you get on, you may not be able to get off ... ever again. <u>Only fully aware Top Choice Bachelors need apply</u>.

The unmentionables

Late-night creeps were made for her; check that, *the late night* was made for her. With this woman, you burn a little more gasoline, drive the extra mile, and eat at restaurants in remote locales at odd times. Why? Because you don't want anyone you know to see you with her. She's a little chunky. Ok, honestly she's a lot of chunky, i.e., fat. There will always be something about her that's "not quite right." Something that makes you not ever want to be seen with her in the daylight hours among the masses. Missing teeth, a lazy eye, or a limp; whatever it is, it's irrelevant because when it's on and you're down, she's around. She can fuck, fuck, fuck. Because as imperfect as her assorted geographic areas may be, the better her pussy is. Big pimples? Big pussy. Busted face? Big pussy. Big gut? Big pussy. And you like it, but will never admit it. Not even to your boys. 3 a.m.? She's open like Sam Goodie and her pussy stays wet. And why? Because she knows that it will be once in a blue moon when you come through to bang and she has to get it when she can.

The holy roller

She claims to be righteous, but in random situations she gets freaky and afterwards will be quick to quote scripture. From Monday to Saturday she sins, only to repent on Sunday and still make it out of church in time for the buffet/happy hour at the local hot spot. She's quick to ridicule other women for their lack of morals, but when she chooses to will break out the stilettos and do the same things they do. When morning comes, she asks herself, "What in Jesus' name did I do?" She says a couple prayers and races home with her Bible cozy in the back seat.

Always remember, men: As your skills progress, so goes the caliber of woman you will ultimately be able to attract. Rarely do you see a herb with a Top Tier chick unless either he is coming heavily out of pocket or something is not quite right with the pair unseen by the naked eye. In these cases, rest assured that at the first moment, she will be stepping out with a Top Choice Bachelor as soon as he buys that overpriced drink. So now that you know, you know exactly what kind of playing field you occupy and what kind of players exist; now what? How high is the caliber of your rifle? How big are your bullets? How sharp are your skills? What kind of woman can you attract? Herb or helluva guy? See month two.

MANTRA: Be able to readily recognize the eight types of women and know which one is right for you.

MONTH 2
Look the part, act the part, and be the part

No woman wants an unconfident man.

It goes to their most primal of urges that you must be "the king of the jungle." The concrete jungle, that is. As a bachelor who plans to be in demand, appearance is everything. Let's start with the shoes. They must be stylish and new, and match your outfit strikingly. Being in the latest fashions is one way to go about it. However, we suggest getting a style that fits you. There is nothing worse than a nerdy-looking guy wearing a throwback jersey and Timberlands. When you find your personal style, own it. Expound on pieces and accessorize. Grooming is a must. We recommend getting a haircut once a week at least, along with a regular manicure and pedicure schedule. Now fellas, we know that sounds kind of "metro," but look at it this way. If a woman knows that you get your nails and feet done more than she does, that can be intimidating. You will eliminate the broke sistas as soon as they find that out. Now remember, you want to be in demand; so keeping appearances up at all times is key.

No woman wants a man another woman does not want.

However, when your wallet does not match your taste, this could become a problem. Remember, you attract who you are. If you cannot afford tailor-made suits, then the chances of you getting a woman in that category is slim. Still, the great thing about black women is that there are fly ones in every category, so upgrade when you can. Looking the part also includes where you live and what you drive. Again, let the car fit your style. Avoid known "female cars." They are a no-go. Honda Civics, Mitsubishi Eclipses, Volkswagen Beetles, Toyota Scions, and the like are "chick cars" unless you're fast and furious. No female wants a man who has the same car her little niece or cousin got for graduation ... don't do it. Make sure your car is clean 90% of the time. Reason? This goes towards your image, for in the female mind, a dirty car equals a dirty house. A dirty house equals dirty sheets. Dirty sheets equal a dirty dick. None of these are acceptable for a Top Choice Bachelor. By the way, fellas, before we leave the subject of cars, rims are optional depending on what you're hunting — refer to month one. Going into debt over rims instead of furnishing your pad is a dumb move.

When choosing your bachelor pad, remember what realtors say: location, location, location. You want to live in a happening part of town. Downtown where the yuppies live is most likely. Look, rent will be extremely high in these areas but remember that you are a Top Choice Bachelor, and living in a kill zone is not playa. Females like to party, and having a place close to the action can be very advantageous for late-night sexual exploits.

Here's a perfect scenario:

She's too drunk to drive? No problem, you live right up the block. This never fails. If you cannot afford a downtown spot, try something off the beaten path. That way, you're still not one of the "run of the mill guys." Let them say, "Wow! You live all the way out here? Damn!" That starts the intrigue about what you have going on, and visiting you will become likened to getting away from it all. They have to damn near pack a lunch for the drive out there. Again, we repeat: It becomes advantageous for late-night sex exploits.

A Second Scenario

"Baby, it's too late for you to drive all the way back home. You could sleep here if you like."

Make sure you have décor that is both contemporary and interesting. Why? Because art is a major turn-on for almost every woman. From Roman Bearden to a picture of Biggie and Tupac at the last supper, give them something to talk about. Remember that cleanliness is very important; if needed, hire a cleaning lady twice a month. It is well worth it. Women hate filth, and they really despise filthy men; that's a major turn-off. Most importantly, have an immaculate kitchen and bathroom. Reason being? These are the rooms that say the most about your cleanliness. Any thirteen-year-old boy can make his bedroom when company is coming over. However, cleaning urine from behind the toilet takes some planning. Make sure your home is female friendly — magazines on the coffee table for them to read when waiting for you to get ready. We suggest *Essence* or *Vanity Fair* and having fruits readily available. Lots of fatty foods and sweets around is a turn-off unless you have kids. Most black women are on some sort of diet so you want to facilitate their healthy eating along with your own.

Having amenities in your domicile or community is also a plus. Hot tubs, pools , saunas, weight rooms, etc. help women to unwind and relax in your presence, which again can lead to you getting to know them a lot faster.

"Looking the part and being the part" means that you want to be in control at all times. You want to appear as a real friend and not some predator who just wants to get between her legs. This is done by being a good listener. Oh yeah, bro', you gotta listen. Black women are very emotional and vivid storytellers, so let them do it. Hell, even ask questions and act shocked during conversations. This will make them feel as though you really give a damn about what they're saying, even if you don't. Examples: "Get outta here! For real!?! That don't make no sense!! They just hatin'!! Don't even sweat that!" These expressions help them to further expound on their issues. After you have heard the whole story, don't be afraid to provide an opinion; women like men who are thinkers and take the initiative in their everyday lives. However, watch yourself. Always be sensible and as "unpreachy" as possible. If a situation arises where they are wrong, don't call them wrong. Never call them wrong. Merely say, "Do you think there was a better way that you could have handled that?" If they say, "No," move on. You do not have time to enhance their analytical skills; you just want to get along for the time being. I also recommend giving them little sayings to think about when they go through things that they inevitability will go through. Example: "Well, baby, everything that's good for you may not be good to you." Also, "Be careful what you ask for, you just may get it." Or, "Lost is the man who gains the world and loses his soul in the process." These quotes will confuse and perplex women oftentimes; yet will let them know that you are an abstract thinker. Women love men who are mysterious and march to the beat of a different drummer. Dare to be different in how you dress, what you drive, and where you live. Have them feel that they have found a friend in you … a fine-dressing, bad-ass car-driving, decked pad living-in friend, who they can't quite figure out. When this happens, just sit back and watch the fun begin.

MANTRA: Concentrate on being the person you want to be and not the person you currently are.

MONTH 3
Money: There's a thin line between being broke and being a damn fool

Money is the root of all evil ... or is it? Allow this to be a nonissue in your relationship. Black women are very money conscious. They stay in tune as to whether you have money or if you're cheap. They know if you don't have money and when you're frontin'.

Always pay for the first date; this is the gentlemanly thing to do. However, be innovative. Do not constantly go on dates that require you to spend a lot of money. Instead, think outside the box. Although they may not know it, women generally want to have a good time, not necessarily an expensive one. In your first conversation with a black woman, throw her off guard. DO NOT talk about money or dollars. DO NOT offer to take care of her. Instead, concentrate on issues of substance, i.e., family, women themselves, their dreams, your dreams, etc. Oftentimes, unknowingly, brothas bring up the issue of money, how much they have, and ultimately how much they are willing to spend. On the flip side, some black women make it very clear that they expect a man to pay for anywhere from 90 – to 100% of the dating expenses. More than ever, it is at this time when *looking the part and acting the part* will become invaluable to you. Once a lady of interest recognizes that she is in the presence of a Top Choice Bachelor, the last thing she wants to do is run him off with her greedy credos. Always give the façade that you are willing to assist them in a financial bind, but at the same time make them feel ashamed to ask a thing of such a cool guy. Never discuss your investments or holdings unless you are willing to break them off with some. In those inevitable times when your profession does come into play during the conversation, focus on the interpersonal element of said job and not the compensation. Your financial status should be as mysterious as the other women she believes exists but has never seen. In the event that you do have a "Beggin' Bonita," weigh your options. Remember, throwing money at a black woman is like throwing water on a grease fire; it will only worsen the situation. Once you open the floodgates of fleecing, you will have to maintain a consistency or it's a letdown to their psyche. Black women feel that the longer they know you and the more frequent your intimate sex sessions, financial upgrades should occur. Start small; this will leave room for growth if you choose. However, if you start to spoil them above your means, you're as good as done. You cannot buy respect or admiration.

SEX IS THE ONLY THING YOU CAN BUY FROM A WOMAN, and even then they will despise you for the monetary hold you possess over them. Remember, every woman who wants to fall in love with your wallet is not always the woman who wants to fall in love with "you the person." However, they do not mind fleecing "Mr. Right Now" while in search of "Mr. Right."

MANTRA: Be smarter with your money and keep your financial situation to yourself.

MONTH 4
You think you're the driver but you're the butler

In the pursuit of sex, men will often get caught up. Men will agonize over a situation such as when a woman has called five or six times a day, thinking that this represents how much she wants to be with you. We mistake <u>distraction</u> for <u>attraction</u>. Don't be fooled, this is merely a ploy used by women in an attempt to make themselves irreplaceable in your life. Women try to find things in which they believe you are lacking and then supply it in hopes that you won't be able to do without it. Thus you will begin to ***need them*** to continue supplying you like a junkie. You must let women know that you are not at their beck and call 24/7 because if you act as "the butler," kowtowing to females on the regular, you will go through a life of kowtowing in your relationships. What is it that you're afraid of losing anyway? Are you afraid of not getting pussy?

Understand this and make this your *modus operandi* — **pussy comes a dime a dozen.**

Pussy comes in all shapes and sizes: fat, wet, dry, black, white, bald, and hairy. The list goes on and on. Pussy broke the president. Men have been taken advantage of by the pursuit of it for centuries, but you like most other men don't understand this because you fear losing access to something you never had in the first place.

The difference between a Top Choice Bachelor and the rest is this. A Top Choice Bachelor knows that whether or not he has lovers at any particular time or another ... pussy will *always* be there. So then we go back to the original question: Are you afraid of losing pussy? Or are you afraid of being alone? Oftentimes fear and uncertainty contribute largely towards men assuming the role of the "butler" and subjecting themselves to buffoon-like acts. Imagining the object of your desire on the arm of another other man (probably a Top Choice Bachelor) can be a jagged pill to swallow. You imagine her laughing at someone else's jokes, joyfully sipping Cosmopolitans, or giving her valuable pussy away to another while you sit at home watching "Sanford and Son" reruns. If these are your thoughts, know this. You've never been the "driver." You're the "butler," and have been the entire time. There is absolutely no need to be compelled to show your friends every five minutes the text messages a woman has sent you. In this case, you're dealing with a woman who is attempting to make herself irreplaceable. She's sending numerous text messages, emails, picture messages, flowers, etc. Whatever it may be, all these things are done in an attempt to ensure that in the event that she becomes upset with you and stops communicating/supplying the item that you are missing, that it will leave a gaping hole in your life and you will do whatever it takes to plug it. Do not be fooled. Do not think that you are so special in that you are different from all the others. However, in the event that you achieve Top Choice Bachelor status, you become special, meaning that you would handle the situation entirely different than most. In the aforementioned case, you must take a stance that any behavior that elicits a favorable response will be duplicated. You must first let them know that those types of tactics neither impress nor excite you. You do not need to be called every day, tracked, or be on a check-in schedule. Men who feel this way are merely being misled.

Example: A veterinarian once had a dog that he conditioned with meat and a bell; each time he rang the bell, the dog would salivate in anticipation of the meat. Concurrently, sometimes a woman will bombard you with "Baby this, baby that. Where you goin? Where you at? Am I bugging you? You busy? When you comin' over? When can I come over?" The moment you allow these kind of questions to become acceptable and you begin to alter your originally scheduled programming, you have already lost. You've been conditioned, just like that vet's dogs were to the bell, now, roll over boy, fetch, and play dead. If you believe this behavior is "cute," you're wrong.

The snow-job has already begun. Walking hand-in-hand every place you go when knowing the only reason you allow it is because you really want sex-capades, but are too afraid to go after it in fear of jeopardizing future pussy that you don't have to begin with. Face it, you're a damn fool! You know you're a damn fool for falling for the ploy, and from that moment on you recognize that you are the "butler." When she calls during a thunderstorm at midnight wanting someone to come over and sit with her and that fuckin' dog that you hate but tolerate in all hopes that this will be the time that actually leads to late-night hype, guess who she calls, Benson? It's you. Now feel special? You never, ever call a woman at the same time every day or go to their home every day. Instead, you need to be unpredictable. This is one of the things women cannot stand. Think about it. If you recall, most of the arguments you've had with the opposite sex surround the same thing: her inability to gauge your predictability. "Where are you? I called you but you didn't answer the phone! I was waiting for you but you never came! I thought you got out of class at six o'clock; what you doin' there at eight o'clock?" Women like to put you in a box, wanting you to be predictable. But you need to understand what most men can't. The same thing that attracted her to you in the first place is what will keep you in the driver's seat. You were a maverick. You were someone who was a challenge to tame. Once you become tame and predictable, my friend, you're as good as done. Or worse, married, living in the suburbs, cutting grass every week, wondering what happened to your life.

MANTRA: Do not be taken advantage of and experience life on your terms.

MONTH 5
Her kids, your burden

The dating landscape is full of "babies mamas." But beware, no matter how much she talks about how "she doesn't need a man," or how "her and her kids will be all right." When she says her kids are "well taken care of," she is usually lying. Mothers love extra stuff: extra money, food, clothes, toilet paper, pens, etc. As a Top Choice Bachelor, you have to put her on the defensive. Let her see that you have a lot of childless female friends. Now this is not meant to make her feel "less than" but for her to know that you are not pressed. In other words, you don't have to put up with her situation due to your being desperate. Black women with kids thrive on desperate men. Desperate men either need a place to stay or a family to love. Some brothers get caught on the "beauty of the specimen," and in turn become all too willing to baby-sit or go to parent/teacher conferences and doctor appointments. Being a Top Choice Bachelor means "never selling the wine before its time." In other words, do not get involved with the kids. Remember you are dating her, not them. Fellas, do not allow her hard-luck stories and your attachment to the kids to dominate you and ruin your rep with the ladies. Nothing will drop your stock around town quicker than taking care of someone else's kids. Bottom line: Mothers should be working overtime to get *your* attention. Why not? They're more inconsistent. The Top Choice Bachelor should always be compensated for inconveniences. Again, place them on the defensive, not vice versa. When they start to gripe about how bad their babies' daddies are treating them and how they can't trust men, reply by saying, "Cool. I feel you." That kind of game on their part is a ploy to make you work hard. You end up spending all your time showing her that you're different while she plays you like a fool. Don't fall into that trap.

MANTRA: Do what is best for you and not for everyone else; do not become a surrogate father unless you want to be.

MONTH 6
Running things means never having to say it

When dealing with the opposite sex, there is always a battle for control. One thing you never get into as a Top Choice Bachelor is a power struggle with a woman, or anyone else, for that matter. Remember, women always feel that in the initial stages of your relationship, it is important for them to flex their independence muscles. Let them. But if they like a man who takes the lead, be prepared to do that too. Remember, being in demand has its privileges. When your lady is not acting in a matter that you appreciate, make her aware of it. If this behavior does not change, merely give her the space that she has asked for. Ration your company. Explain to her that her behavior and how often she sees you are directly correlated. Now, don't get us wrong; some women will say "my way or no way" and be fine with not hearing from you because of their pride. That's absolutely fine. As we mentioned, everyone will not be buying what you're selling. Some women are looking for suckers and will not accept anything except a sucker. You are in control. Eligible black women outnumber eligible black men in every major city in this country. You must use this to your advantage. There is no need to say, "You better do this" or "Do that." Simply convey that if they cannot meet your needs, you will have to look for someone more compatible with your personality. Again, keep the pressure on them and not on yourself. Do not be rude or cruel about the situation, and be sure to highlight all of their good qualities. Yet add, "However, this part of your personality needs to be addressed." Now they may try to flip the script on you but don't fall for this. Reiterate that this may not be fair but it is how you roll, and in rolling with you, she must note that your pluses far out weigh your minuses. End of story.

Being a Top Choice Bachelor doesn't come without its drawbacks. To women, you're a strange bird. Not chasing after women, like the majority of the species, will only vilify you to the opposite sex. She will be totally befuddled that you give her all the room she needs, yet you still maintain a laissez-faire attitude about your relationship. The average sista will want to get an emotional rise out of you either for her own ego or to see how much you care. This is not to be fallen for. When she is overwhelmed by her inability to cope with you entertaining other "friends" of the female gender or she is infuriated by the amount of time you allow her to spend with you (when she has not proven herself worthy of spending more of it with you), simply allow her to vent. Now let's clarify that. Any public displays of angst such as loud talking or the use of profane language and the like should be walked away from immediately. Simply get up, head to your mode of transportation, and go home. If she rode with you, be sure to leave her cab fare in a calm manner and leave. The goal of many women who see a man in control of his emotions is to pierce his armor, e.g., make you lose your cool. Remember, *you* choose to get angry, upset, or out of control. She has no control over your behavior. If an altercation ignites in your apartment, be firm in letting her know you have neighbors and aggressive behavior will not be tolerated; even to the point of you calling the authorities. A lot of these situations can be avoided by really examining the women you choose to date. Date only the best, a woman who really has it going on in the areas of career, looks, *and* mentality. A woman well-connected in these three areas is less likely to act in an uncouth manner. However, if you have a woman with low self-esteem who is mediocre in her achievement status, then she will start to see you as the focal point in her life. This will cause her to lash out if she thinks you are not playing by her rules. Remember: "Garbage in, garbage out." In other words, you get out what you put in. Just because a woman wanted to give you some pussy does not mean she is playing with a full deck. Be careful, many women are emotionally scarred and get easily attached. Always be straight up in how you stand in the relationship. In other words, <u>don't sell these crazy ho's any dreams</u>. Then they won't act a fool. But if they do, be cool. Don't raise your voice. And for god's sake, no matter what happens, what is said, broken, scratched, or flattened, <u>NEVER PUT YOUR HANDS ON A WOMAN</u>. No hitting, slapping, or even holding their arms. All of the aforementioned things guarantee that your name will be mud when you are arrested. Game over if that happens; she got the best of you. Do not fall victim to someone who wants you so much that they start to hate you. Instead, cause them to hate the fact that they don't have what it takes to keep you. Remember, you are a Top Choice Bachelor. You require the best, not the rest.

MANTRA: When faced with an adverse situation, remain calm, quiet, and concise.

MONTH 7
Keep her guessing

Being a Top Choice Bachelor means always being in demand. Never shy away from letting a love interest know that she is not alone in wanting your affection. Now, don't get us wrong, we don't mean saying it verbally. Actions speak louder than words. Drama is what life is made of; however, not the negative type that people often associate with the word. Make your woman be in "competition mode" from time to time. Remember, no woman wants a man that other women don't. Have parties and invite your "friends," both male and female, and play host. Let your ladies see their competition; this will only make them want you more. Avoid treating any one of them more special than the others. This will continue to make each lady feel she has an equal chance to win your affections. When asked, "Who the hell is that chick?" play coy and say, "Oh, Jane Doe, she's one of my friends." And leave it at that: no long talk, no explanations. If at any time a female suitor becomes rowdy or rude, let her know that if she intends on disrespecting your party, she will be asked to leave.

As far as your lady friends visiting you, make it very clear that pop-up visits will not be entertained (see month twelve on apartment/house styles). Entry gates and front desk people come in handy with overanxious females. Remember, women are emotional and oftentimes act without the benefit of intellect. Do not allow them to suck you into an uncool scene. Always tell them straight up you are dating. The names are not important but your privacy is. This will deter them from wanting to pop up, because they know they don't have a leg to stand on in a confrontation. In the event that your ladies do meet up in public, be cool, introduce them to each other, and keep it moving. Never look shocked or avoid eye contact. Welcome the chance meeting and let them both see that you are the man the ladies want to be with. This is just another one of many potentially hairy situations that go along with the territory. If you see your lady friend at the club with someone else, don't lose your cool by doing things out of character like dancing too close to your dance partner or approaching her and asking, "Who's this?" Remember, you must maintain a certain standard of cool. Act normal, drink what you regularly drink, don't buy champagne just to make your other lady friend jealous. This will only send the wrong message to the lady you are with, and what is that message? That she is special to you. Ladies think that if you are displaying attention-seeking behavior, then you must really be feeling them, and this is the moment you go from being the hunter to the hunted, which is the wrong place to be. Remember, you are a Top Choice Bachelor; the prize, the ring, and the life. No drama is too much for a lady to believe she has a chance at becoming "The Mrs." Understand this point and let it ooze through every pore of your body.

MANTRA: Do not allow yourself to get comfortable in the comfort zone; actively seek perfection.

MONTH 8
Do what other brothers won't and go where they don't

Rarely does loud music and ass-shaking with 100 of

your closest friends produce relationships with a shelf life

of more than a couple hours. Many men fall victim to

the cycle of monotony when it comes to dating. From

A to Z, men use the same cachet of places and things

to attempt to impress the opposite sex: movie, dinner at

an all-too-popular restaurant, a concert, maybe a game.

After one, maybe two times through the rotation with

the occasional reshuffling of events, everyone is bored

senseless and the question of "What to do next?" arises.

Remember the month and the mantra. You aspire to be a Top Choice Bachelor, and in doing so you should have at your disposal a vast repertoire of activities that you can access, either day or night; having this will not only associate you with originality in her memory but also sets you apart from any other men from here to eternity. Try this as step 1: Pick up a newspaper, turn to the entertainment or society sections, and see what of interest is available to you. This does two things: (1) It gives you the opportunity to be knowledgeable on a multitude of subjects, and (2) It allows you to broaden her horizons to events off the beaten path. Instead of a tired movie, go to the museum. Worn-out restaurant? Try dinner at a chic eating establishment chased with an evening poetry reading downtown. Concert? Try a play. And why a play, you ask? Because it guarantees you the opportunity to elicit conversation afterwards, with the possibility of a nightcap and not the ringing of your ears and hours of traffic that a concert would guarantee you. Game? Go on an evening stroll through a nice, well-lit park or arboretum armed with a bottle of wine, cheese, and a blanket. For those of you who don't know, an arboretum is a well-manicured area of beautiful trees, shrubs, and walking trails. Before you ask, no, it is not the same as the woods. Do your research. Tired movie? Take her wine tasting instead; you'll come out about even in price and will avoid overpriced snack foods, thus expanding your mind as well your taste palate. Step 2: It has been said that music soothes the savage beast and in this respect women are no different. Smooth grooves and mellow ambiance make unrivaled conduits for verbal exchanges between the Top Choice Bachelor and the opposite sex. Seek out establishments that feature live music with actual musicians over places that play prerecorded drivel at undesirable volumes. If you are not a fan of live music, become one, and quickly. An effective strategy is to frequent these places even if you are not a lover of this genre of music. You will be provided with a preset opportunity to sit back and relax in a setting with low lighting and mellow bystanders; most importantly, you will have both room to enjoy your company and to converse over libations without the worry of having them spilled on her and having the memory of that associated with you in her mind forever.

A definite must for men is to "get to know yourself by yourself," meaning that it's usually a good idea for you to know your likes and dislikes before you attempt to impress the opposite sex with events that you know absolutely nothing about. That has in the past proven to be a waste of time and energy. If you don't read, by all means try to, from time to time. To many men, books prove intimidating, and if this is the case with you, we suggest trying to read smaller books with short chapters on subjects of both interest to you and actual substance. If unable to finish the book, at least know enough to elicit conversation when discussing subjects it concerns. Magazines help also. Allow yourself pockets of time set aside for you and no one else; when phones ring or emails arrive, set them aside until your personal time is over. The majority of your day should not solely be dominated with activities designed to stifle your time. At least two to four hours of every day should be dedicated to you alone; your time is a gift given only when you see fit — use it as such. In your personal time, sharpen both your body and mind to new and stimulating things that interest you and ensure that when the time comes, you will have further distanced yourself from the pack of potential pursuers. Whatever those things may be, ensure the new additions to the collective are worthwhile. In the event that you see fit to share portions of your knowledge base of diverse topics and activities with others, they, as well as you, will be better for it. Enjoy.

MANTRA: Be unique and innovative about where you choose to spend your time.

MONTH 9
Winning the "friend" game

When we get into this lovely world of the "friend,"
the word "friend" can take on many meanings. A friend
can be someone of the same sex that we just like to hang
around with. Like the old saying "home girl" or "home
boy," we go to games with this person, gossip, play sports,
and generally have a good time. Then there is the opposite-
sex friend, which at times can have the same attributes as
the same-sex friend; however, in those types of situations,
the friendship usually goes back to childhood. When
opposite-sex individuals are friends in their adult years,

the chance for romance always exists. FYI, don't be fooled. This brings us to our favorite classification of friend: the "booty-buddy." When you are dealing with a female and she says she has "friends," this means guys she fucks but they have no claim to her. For example, she goes out with you on a date and is turned on, she may feel it is too early to break you off. In those cases when you leave, she calls her "friend" *Dick on the spot;* he is always ready to get down whenever she calls and has no problem not speaking to her for weeks until he gets that call again. As we have been saying throughout this book, keep your emotions out of things. When a lady says she has friends, leave it at that. Do not fall into the trap of trying to possess her to the point that all she wants is you. Remember, the more you pull, the more they will push you away. You are a Top Choice Bachelor, do not chase her. If you've been handling your business, then your harem should be where it needs to be to the degree that you are never pressed or desperate. In winning this game, the key is to be you. Have her just enjoy your company to the extent that she wants more and more of it. When this happens, you remind her that you guys are friends and you really did not think she was interested in being more than that. This will keep the pressure to change her lifestyle on her and not you. If you want this lady as your steady, it is imperative that she understands that many women love your company and you are in no rush to choose. This will make being your main girl a challenge and something she has had to work for. The booty buddies that she has may have become more of a hindrance than a help. You will notice the all-too-familiar sign when this change is taking place: She will begin to call you more and attempt to make plans earlier in the week with regularity. If she is the common woman, she will also begin to press you about your "friends" and whereabouts when she cannot reach you. However, she has made no mention of wanting to be exclusive. In these cases, play dumb; make her spell out exactly what she wants. This way, she will never feel coaxed into lockdown because she came to you willingly. Fellas, however, we warn you: If you do not want her as your girl, do not take the aforementioned approach. Let her do her, and you do you. Become one of her booty buddies and call it a wrap. However, if you do want her, live your life. Let her know that you cannot meet her at the bar, you have a prior engagement. This way, she will understand that your time is valuable and you are not the average desperado she's used to.

MANTRA: Treat people according to who they are, not as you wish them to be.

MONTH 10
Know when to bow out gracefully

In this wacky world of dating, so many men are willing to disrespect themselves for female attention. It is, in a word, ridiculous. Some woman have been spoiled all their life by herbs. These fools can make it easy or hard for you. No matter how charming, attractive, and great her personality is, a woman may say, "My way or the highway." This usually concerns a money issue. Some women require you to support, sport, pay, trick, splurge, and pamper them. You are a top Choice Bachelor; you are more than capable of bedazzling her with all the previously mentioned requisites given the opportunity, but you won't. In case you are propositioned by this kind of woman, do not be afraid to bow out gracefully. Some women seek out suckers. They have such unassuming ways of making "it" sound, "it" being the "herb turnout," that is. They will try and make you second-guess yourself as if to ask the question, "Why am I not getting with her?" "She's so damn fly and shit!" "And cool too!!" Like there's something wrong with <u>you</u> or something! Instead of bending over to get fucked like the new piece of ass at the penitentiary, do not take the common route and try to change them. That would be like trying to make a drug dealer go legit. They have to change on their own. In this kind of situation, these things should prompt you to leave the chick alone and let her find the herb she wants. This is not a negative reflection on you; even if you have a million dollars to merely give to a woman for her company, this insinuates that her attributes are worth paying for and that your *only* attribute is money. Fellas, we are better that that. However, low self-esteem is rampant among men whether they admit or not. We don't want you to base your worth on the women you get. You are a Top Choice Bachelor. However, if you are not comfortable spending time by yourself, you will always be taken advantage of by a woman. If a particular woman is not buying what you're selling, fine; leave it alone. Sometimes, women will see a seasoned veteran and play hard just to make you work. We call this "flipping the script." That way, you will think she is the one because she did not fall for your charm and style straight off. My Top Choice Bachelor buddies, this is how you get roped into marriage. She knew all along she wanted you; however, she ran down a game on your mind to make you believe she was actually doing *you* a favor. She even held back on the sex so you thought she was pure and not a freak, not knowing she had a "friend" serving her up once a month. However, she had the whole game figured out because you had too much pride to bow out gracefully. Again, when you become the hunted instead of the hunter, the balance of power will swing. Be in love with your own company; this will only make you a stronger person. If marriage is in your future, she will be willing to put her cards out on the table and ask you to do the same. At that point, you have to decide what you want to do.

MANTRA: Do not allow your ego to cloud your better judgment.

MONTH 11
Keep your lips closed while keeping hers open

It is very important for a Top Choice Bachelor to be as discreet as possible in matters of the heart. The first rule is never tell your male companions what you are doing romantically, or who you are doing it with. Now, we know this may not make for great male bonding, but there are well-thought-out reasons behind this. Loose lips sink ships. Your boys will be the first ones to hate, cock-block, or just plain fuck up your game. Especially if your female friend is friends with his female friend. Oftentimes he may be pumped for information about you by his girlfriend solely for the purposes of her telling your lady. What your friends don't know they cannot tell. Don't be mistaken. Do not lie to your boys, simply let them know your business is yours alone and you care not to discuss it. If they have things going for themselves, they won't have any problem accepting your stance. Another reason you never talk about the woman you're seeing is that women like to feel as though if they do something with you, no one else will ever know. They can be the freak they always wanted to be with you. It is very important they know that there are things that only the two of you share. Now if you are the stud every Top Choice Bachelor should be, she will spread news of your prowess in the bedroom. Her other friends will either approach you or act funny around you. Woman love to see and experience anyone who has been confirmed as "fucks well." Don't be fooled, never admit to anything. If you do, her girlfriends will know they could never fuck you simply because you have a big mouth. It is very possible for you to have sex with her whole entire clique, but only if they are certain you will never share information with another living soul. Keep your exploits to yourself and hang on for the ride.

MANTRA: Keep your personal life personal.

MONTH 12
Bring your "A" game

Your verbal prowess provides a preview to both your intellect and the possibility that you may be able to back those sweet words up with some sweet dick, so let's be honest. In the arena of the Top Choice Bachelor, "talking a good game" and then backing that game up is key in the establishment of you over everyone else. Women use their gift of cunning to their advantage all the time: makeup, lip gloss, eye shadow, sexually suggestive clothing accentuating their lady lumps. Why can't a man use his gifts as well? You can use your masculinity, prowess (both physical and verbal), and conversation, etc. Conversation gives insight into what you bring to the table and what you have to offer.

The void between "spittin' game" and having worthwhile conversation is vast, and the man who can navigate this void is king. Indeed, the Top Choice Bachelor is that man. The art of conversation is a skill needing to be honed in the arena of life. In order to exercise your conversational muscle, you must have real-life experiences. For those not gifted with a well-endowed mouthpiece, one must learn how to cope. Here's a suggestion: Think before you speak. Nothing provides a kill to a promising verbal exchange quite like a dumb-ass line or a poorly thought-out attempt at conversational stimulation. Before you open your mouth and embarrass yourself, have an idea on what you'll talk about, and observe your desired one to determine what you're going to talk about. Follow these easy directions. (1) State the obvious: Simplicity is bliss; if well-dressed, compliment her on that without being verbose or crass. (2) Remain brief; nobody digs a "jabber jaw"; build an aura of intrigue about you that stimulates her mind and entices her to want to know more. (3) Stand firm; no need to act needy. Remember, you're a Top Choice Bachelor. Display yourself as cool, conversational, and educated. Act as if beautiful women are a dime a dozen with you, even when they are not. Offer chase only when necessary and never give up the mantle of flyness by chasing some chicken-head around a club all night. If the object of your desire is requesting too much pursuit in order to seal the deal, then stop running, both literally and figuratively. <u>And for god's sake, put your money back in your pocket!</u>

You're a man, not an ATM! Buying sour apple martinis or whipping your plastic out at the drop of a hat to pay for meals does not reveal or promote flyness. Instead, it's an advertisement for a sucker, so put your "game" and your wallet back in your pocket, Romeo, before you hurt yourself.

Gone are the days of a man paying for everything without question. This is the twenty-first century, and chivalry may not be dead but it sure as hell has gotten an education. What that means is this: You do not buy every drink for every "naggin' Nancy" that smiles at you. She can pay her own way, this is not the March of Dimes. No one is saying for you to become a miser and not bring your wallet out with you. What is being stated is the obvious: Don't introduce yourself as the guy who supplies funds before any conversation has been exchanged. Be selective and don't spend your good coin on every ass that smiles. When the evening changes scenes from public (restaurants, nightclubs, walks in the park) to private (your place or her place), the Top Choice Bachelor is never caught off-guard. Like a well-trained athlete on his field of play, you are at home. Not only must you be fly in your outward presentation (dress, car, etc.), your domicile must be on par with your dress. Remember, stay classy not assy when it comes to the place where you lay your head (see month two). There is nothing wrong with using color in your home to accent stylish furniture and floor plans. Try something different other than having a black sofa or black chairs or black everything else. Instead, go with peanut butter or assorted earth tones. Soft lighting draws attention to angles and artwork — yes, artwork. Show that not only do you look good but you have an eye for *what* looks good as well. The Top Choice Bachelor also knows that the kitchen is actually used to cook entrees, often by the use of the range and not solely the microwave oven. Preparing meals that not only look good but taste good adds a dimension that few can match and even fewer can successfully achieve. Become comfortable around the cutting board. When entertaining company on occasion, do so from the kitchen. It gives a sense of inclusion and warmth; food channels or food shows are your friends. Producing masterpieces with your own hands shows the woman that you have an ability to pay attention to detail, and in doing so you will create delicious dishes while having another delicious dish eating out of the palm of your hand.

So there you have it; everything a man needs to go

from herb to helluva guy. You have all the mantras in hand to keep you in focus, should you think with the head on your shoulder and not the one in your trousers. If followed, this guide will transform the dating scene into your personal playground complete with many new playmates. And why? Because you now see with different eyes: the eyes of a Top Choice Bachelor, able to see different people, personalities, and situations as they *really* are. Simply put, you will be wanted by all, hated by many, and selective of a few. Now go get 'em. Welcome to the coalition.

MANTRA: Become the Top Choice Bachelor: mind, body, and soul